RECIPES

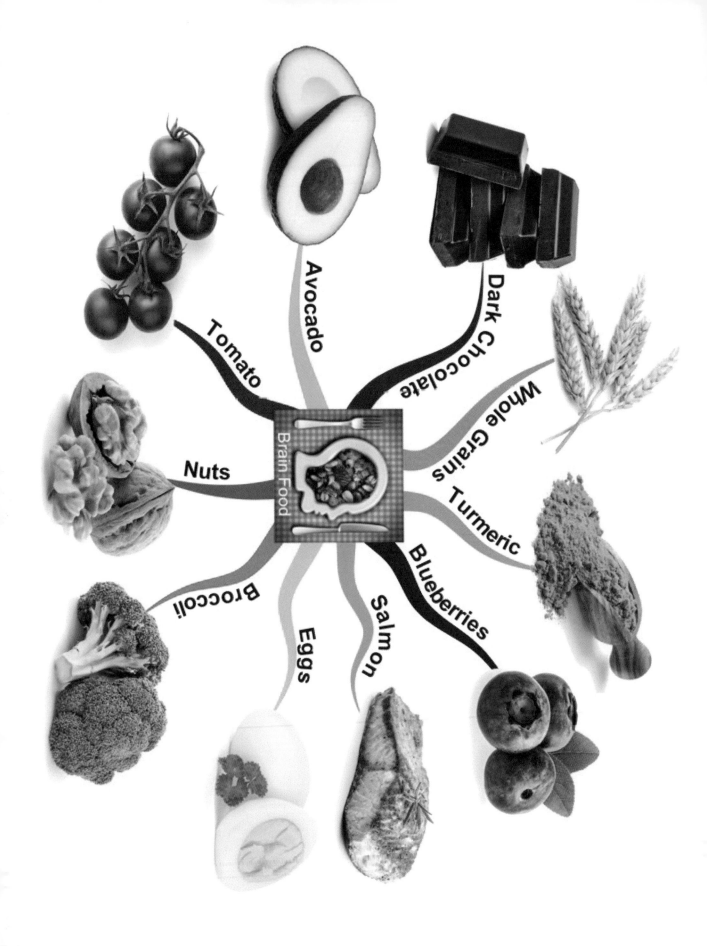

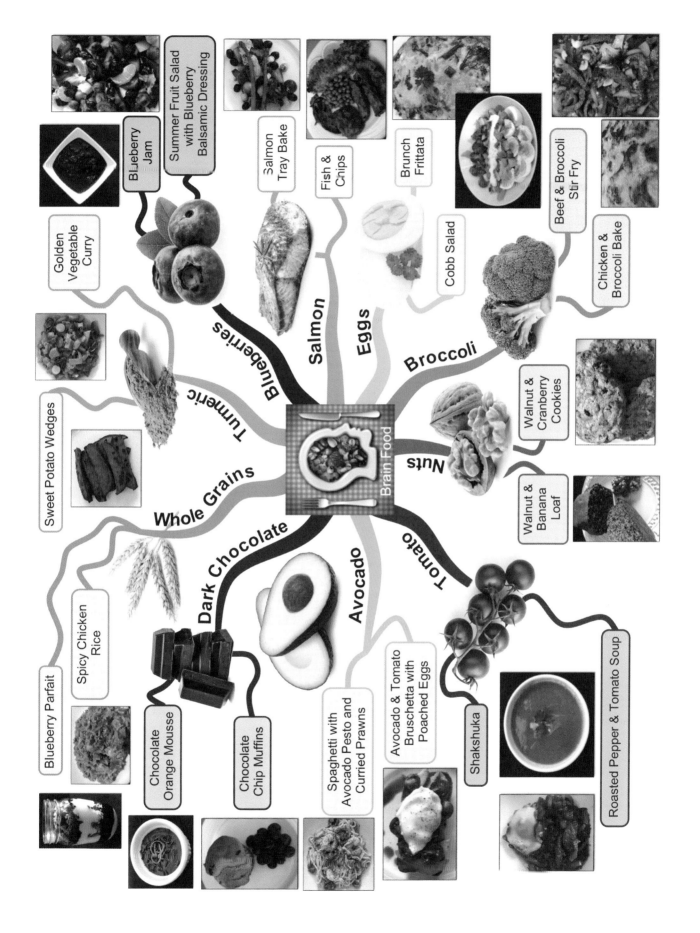

Brain Food

- Blueberries
  - Blueberry Jam
  - Summer Fruit Salad with Blueberry Balsamic Dressing
  - Golden Vegetable Curry
- Salmon
  - Salmon Tray Bake
  - Fish & Chips
- Eggs
  - Brunch Frittata
  - Cobb Salad
- Broccoli
  - Beef & Broccoli Stir Fry
  - Chicken & Broccoli Bake
- Nuts
  - Walnut & Cranberry Cookies
  - Walnut & Banana Loaf
- Tomato
  - Shakshuka
  - Roasted Pepper & Tomato Soup
- Avocado
  - Avocado & Tomato Bruschetta with Poached Eggs
  - Spaghetti with Avocado Pesto and Curried Prawns
- Dark Chocolate
  - Chocolate Orange Mousse
  - Chocolate Chip Muffins
- Whole Grains
  - Blueberry Parfait
  - Spicy Chicken Rice
- Turmeric
  - Sweet Potato Wedges

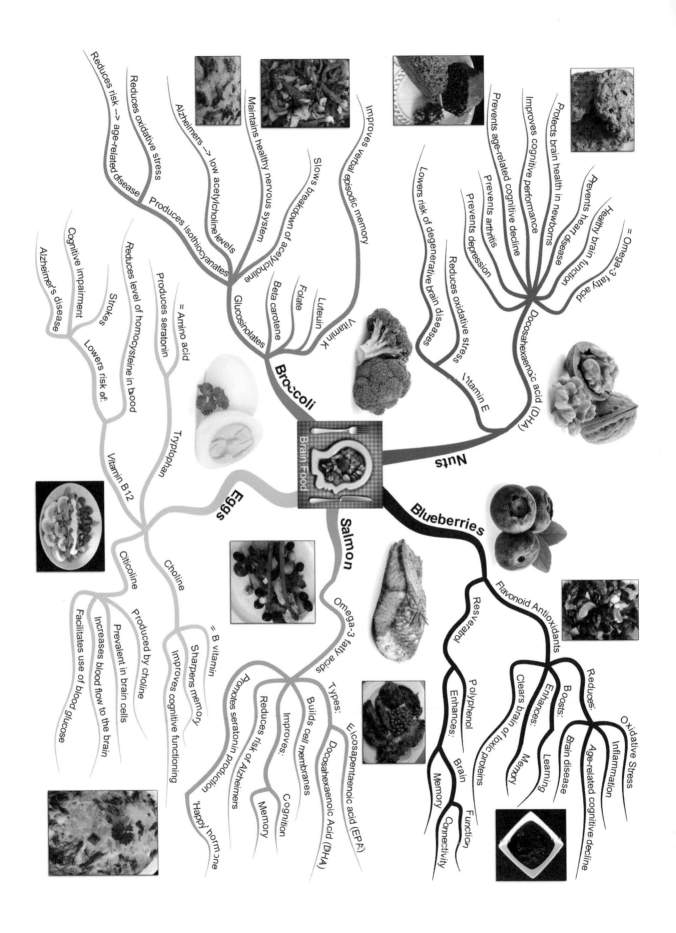

Brain Food

Broccoli

- Improves verbal episodic memory
- Maintains healthy nervous system
- Alzheimers → low acetylcholine levels
  - Slows breakdown of acetylcholine
- Produces isothiocyanates
  - Reduces oxidative stress
  - Reduces risk → age-related disease
- Glucosinolates
  - Beta carotene
  - Folate
  - Luteuin
  - = Vitamin K

Nuts

- Docosahexaenoic acid (DHA)
  - Lowers risk of degenerative brain diseases
  - Reduces oxidative stress
  - = Vitamin E
- = Omega-3 fatty acid
  - Healthy brain function
  - Prevents heart disease
  - Protects brain health in newborns
  - Improves cognitive performance
  - Prevents age-related cognitive decline
  - Prevents arthritis
  - Prevents depression

Eggs

- = Amino acid
  - Produces seratonin
  - Reduces level of homocysteine in blood
    - Lowers risk of:
      - Alzheimer's disease
      - Cognitive impairment
      - Strokes
  - Tryptophan
- Vitamin B12
- Choline
- Citicoline
  - Produced by choline
  - Prevalent in brain cells
  - Increases blood flow to the brain
  - Facilitates use of blood glucose
  - Improves cognitive functioning
  - Sharpens memory
  - = B vitamin

Salmon

- Omega-3 fatty acids
  - Promotes seratonin production
    - 'Happy' hormone
  - Reduces risk of Alzheimers
  - Improves:
    - Memory
    - Cognition
  - Builds cell membranes
  - Types:
    - Docosahexaenoic Acid (DHA)
    - Eicosapentaenoic acid (EPA)

Blueberries

- Flavonoid Antioxidants
  - Resveratrol
    - Polyphenol
    - Enhances:
      - Brain
      - Memory
      - Function
      - Connectivity
    - Clears brain of toxic proteins
  - Enhances:
    - Memory
    - Learning
  - Boosts:
    - Brain disease
    - Age-related cognitive decline
  - Reduces:
    - Oxidative Stress
    - Inflammation

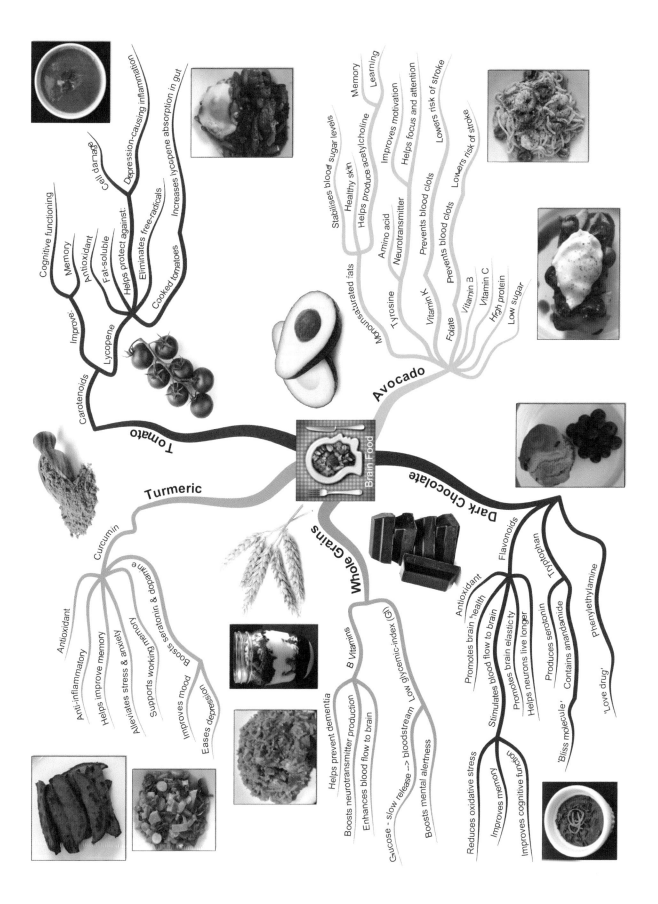

Brain Food

Tomato
Carotenoids
Lycopene
Improve:
Cognitive functioning
Memory
Antioxidant
Fat-soluble
Helps protect against:
Cell damage
Depression-causing inflammation
Eliminates free-radicals
Cooked tomatoes
Increases lycopene absorption in gut

Avocado
Monounsaturated fats
Stabilises blood sugar levels
Healthy skin
Helps produce acetylcholine
Memory
Learning
Improves motivation
Helps focus and attention
Lowers risk of stroke
Amino acid
Neurotransmitter
Tyrosine
Vitamin K
Prevents blood clots
Prevents blood clots
Lowers risk of stroke
Folate
Vitamin 3
Vitamin C
High protein
Low sugar

Turmeric
Curcumin
Antioxidant
Anti-inflammatory
Helps improve memory
Alleviates stress & anxiety
Supports working memory
Boosts seratonin & dopamine
Improves mood
Eases depression

Whole Grains
B Vitamins
Helps prevent dementia
Boosts neurotransmitter production
Enhances blood flow to brain
Glucose - slow release --> bloodstream
Low glycemic-index (GI)
Boosts mental alertness

Dark Chocolate
Flavonoids
Antioxidant
Promotes brain health
Stimulates blood flow to brain
Promotes brain elasticity
Helps neurons live longer
Reduces oxidative stress
Improves memory
Improves cognitive function
Tryptophan
Produces serotonin
'Bliss molecule'
Contains anandamide
Phenylethylamine
'Love drug'

Blueberries

Boosts short-term memory

Blueberries contain flavonoid antioxidants, including anthocyanin, caffeic acid, catechin, and quercetin. The anthocyanins give blueberries their rich blue colour.

Antioxidants have several health benefits for the brain. Specifically, they help to reduce oxidative stress and inflammation, boost learning, enhance memory and reduce/delay age-related cognitive decline and brain disease. Eating blueberries helps to protect the brain against Alzheimer's and Parkinson's disease by clearing the brain of toxic proteins. A recent study showed that a group of adults with mild cognitive impairment experienced improved memory and better brain functioning by eating the equivalent of 100g of blueberries per day for sixteen weeks.

Blueberries also contain resveratrol, a polyphenol also found in red wine. Resveratrol is referred to as 'the fountain of youth' and is linked to enhanced brain function, memory and brain connectivity in the elderly.

Summer Salad with Blueberry Balsamic Dressing

Fresh, fruity and packed with flavour

Serves 4

Ingredients:

100g blueberries
Mixed salad leaves - washed
½ cucumber – chopped
16 cherry tomatoes
24 mandarin orange segments
40g dried cranberries
2 tablespoons sunflower seeds

Balsamic Dressing:
100g blueberries
100ml balsamic vinegar
2 tablespoons red wine vinegar
1 tablespoon maple syrup
1 teaspoon salt
120ml extra virgin olive oil

Method:

1. Make the balsamic dressing by blending together the blueberries, balsamic vinegar, red wine vinegar, syrup and salt in a food processor. Slowly pour the extra virgin olive oil into the puree until thoroughly combined.
2. Toss the mixed salad leaves, cucumber and tomatoes in a salad bowl.
3. Top with the mandarin segments, cranberries and sunflower seeds.
4. Drizzle the salad with the balsamic dressing and serve.

Serving Suggestions:

- Serve with warm wholegrain brain or boiled baby potatoes.
- Add slices of smoked salmon or prawns.
- To make a thinner dressing, add more oil to achieve the desired consistency.

Blueberry Jam

Delicious served with warm wholegrain bread

Serves 6

Ingredients:

400g blueberries
Grated zest of ½ lemon
2 tablespoons maple syrup
2 tablespoons chia seeds

Method:

1. Gently simmer the blueberries in a small pan for 8-10 minutes until the blueberries start to release juice. Stir regularly.
2. Bring to the boil.
3. Remove from the heat and mash the fruit to make a chunky puree.
4. Add the maple syrup and lemon zest and cook for 5 minutes. Stir regularly.
5. Stir in the chia seeds and continue to cook the jam for 5-10 minutes until it starts to thicken. The jam will still be runny because it only thickens once it starts to cool. Note: the more chia seeds added to the mixture, the thicker the jam.
6. Taste and add more maple syrup to sweeten.
7. Cool and store in the refrigerator for up to 1 week.

Serving Suggestions:

- Spread onto warm wholegrain bread for a delicious breakfast.
- Serve with dark chocolate pancakes topped with fresh berries.
- Use in the blueberry parfait recipe on page 41.

Salmon

Promotes healthy brain function

Oily fish, including salmon, are a good source of omega-3 fatty acids in the form of eicosapentaenoic acid (EPA), and Docosahexaenoic Acid (DHA). The body cannot make these fatty acids, so it is necessary to obtain them through a diet rich in omega-3.

Omega-3's help build the membranes around cells in the body and improve the structure of neurons. Studies have shown a correlation between the levels of omega-3 and improved cognition, including better memory. In fact, the University of Pittsburgh showed that adults under the age of 25 improved their performance on tests designed to measure their working memory when they increased their intake of omega-3's.

Low DHA levels may increase the risk of dementia in old age. Research shows that eating oily fish once a week can reduce the risk of Alzheimer's by up to 70%. Furthermore, maintaining sufficient levels of EPA and DHA helps to manage stress and promotes the production of the 'happy hormone' serotonin.

Salmon Traybake

A quick and easy mid-week fish supper

Serves 4

Ingredients:

4 salmon fillets
2 tablespoons extra virgin olive oil
500g new potatoes – halved
2 red onions – sliced
150g mange tout – trimmed
150g cherry tomatoes
150g sweetcorn – cut into small chunks
1 lemon – zest and juice
1 teaspoon dill
200g black olives
8 asparagus tips
Salt and black pepper

Method:

1. Preheat oven to 180°C/160° Fan/Gas 4.
2. Heat the extra virgin olive oil in a large roasting tin. When the oil is hot, add the potatoes and roast for 15 minutes.
3. Add the onions and roast for 10 minutes.
4. Place the salmon fillets between the potatoes and onions and add the mange tout, tomatoes, sweetcorn and olives.
5. Drizzle the salmon with the dill, lemon juice and lemon zest and season well.
6. Roast for 15 minutes until the salmon is cooked through.
7. Meanwhile, steam the asparagus tips over a pan of boiling water for 5 minutes until tender.
8. Lay the asparagus tips on top of the salmon and serve.

Fish and Chips

Delicious oven-baked salmon with tomato sauce

Serves 2

Ingredients:

2 salmon fillets – boneless and skinless
4 slices of wholegrain bread – very lightly toasted
2 eggs
½ lemon

Tomato Sauce:
1 tbsp extra virgin olive oil
1 onions – finely diced
1 garlic clove - crushed
1 tablespoon tomato purée
1 x 400g cans chopped tomatoes
1 teaspoon dried mixed herbs

Method:

1. Preheat oven to 180°C/160° Fan/Gas 4.
2. Make the tomato sauce: Heat the olive oil and add the onions and sauté with the garlic until soft. Stir in the tomato purée and cook on a low heat for 2 minutes. Add the tomatoes and herbs and season well. Simmer for 20 minutes. Cool before serving.
3. Place the bread slices into a food processor and process to make medium-sized breadcrumbs. Tip into a shallow dish.
4. Whisk the eggs and pour into a shallow dish.
5. Dip the salmon into the egg and coat thoroughly.
6. Next, coat the salmon on both sides with the breadcrumbs.
7. Place the salmon onto a pre-heated non-stick baking tray and bake in the oven for 15 minutes or until the breadcrumbs are golden brown.
8. Serve with a portion of peas, a slice of lemon, tomato sauce and Spicy Potato Wedges (recipe on page 44).

Eggs

Eating eggs can make you happy!

Eggs are a rich source of choline - a B vitamin-like nutrient - which is a precursor of acetylcholine, a neurotransmitter involved with memory and learning. It is critical for a sharp memory and cognitive functioning. Studies have shown a link between low levels of acetylcholine and Alzheimer's disease.

Choline also produces the brain nutrient, citicoline. Citicoline is prevalent in brain cells, and its role is to increase blood flow to the brain and facilitate the use of blood glucose, which is its primary fuel source.

Eggs also contain tryptophan, which is an amino acid used in the production of the neurotransmitter serotonin, the 'happiness molecule'. They are also packed with protein, vitamin B12, vitamin D, and are a good source of omega-3 fatty acids. Vitamin B12 is known to reduce levels of homocysteine in the blood, which helps to lower the risk of stroke, cognitive impairment and Alzheimer's disease. Furthermore, people who suffer from a lack of vitamin D in their diet may experience faster rates of mental decline than those who have an adequate intake of vitamin D.

Brunch Frittata

A nutritious brunch packed with goodness

Serves 2

Ingredients:

Smoked salmon trimmings
6 asparagus spears – chopped
100g broccoli florets
2 spring onions - chopped
50g cheddar cheese – grated
6 large eggs
1 tablespoon extra virgin olive oil

Method:

1. Preheat oven to 200°C/180° Fan/Gas 6.
2. Crack the eggs into a large bowl and whisk.
3. Combine the eggs with the salmon, asparagus, spring onions and cheese.
4. Fry the broccoli in an ovenproof frying pan for 3 minutes.
5. Add the egg mixture and cook for 2 minutes.
6. Bake in the oven for 10-12 minutes until the eggs are cooked and the frittata is golden brown on top.
7. Turn the frittata onto a plate and serve with a green salad.

Cobb Salad

Boost your brainpower with this tasty lunch

Serves 2

Ingredients:

Lettuce leaves – shredded
3 rashers bacon – cooked and sliced
1 avocado - sliced
2 eggs – boiled and sliced
150g cooked chicken - sliced
¼ cucumber - chopped
6 cherry tomatoes - halved
1 tablespoon chopped chives
2 basil leaves – chopped
Sesame seeds

Dressing:
75ml Greek yogurt
2 tablespoons mayonnaise
½ garlic clove - crushed
½ tablespoon white wine vinegar
1 teaspoon dried chives

Method:

1. Shred the lettuce and place into a bowl.
2. Arrange the tomatoes, cucumber, chicken, bacon and avocado on top of the lettuce.
3. Add the sliced egg.
4. In a small bowl, whisk the yogurt, mayonnaise, garlic, vinegar and chives until combined.
5. Serve the dressing with the salad.
6. Sprinkle the salad with the chopped basil leaves and sesame seeds.

Serving Suggestions:

• Substitute the chicken and bacon for salmon and prawns.
• Use pumpkin seeds or pine nuts instead of the sesame seeds.

Broccoli

The ultimate brain food

Broccoli is a cruciferous vegetable that is rich in brain-healthy nutrients including vitamin K, lutein, folate, and beta carotene.

Broccoli is high in compounds called glucosinolates, which slow the breakdown of the neurotransmitter, acetylcholine, which is required to maintain a healthy nervous system and to optimise the functioning of the brain. Alzheimer's patients have low levels of acetylcholine, so it is vital to eat a diet rich in vegetables containing glucosinolates. In fact, studies show that people who consume one or two servings of glucosinolate-rich foods every day have fewer memory problems and cognitive decline than people who rarely eat green vegetables.

Glucosinolates are broken down in the body to produce isothiocyanates which have been shown to reduce oxidative stress and reduce the risk of age-related, neurodegenerative diseases. Furthermore, broccoli is a good source of vitamin K, which is known to Improve verbal episodic memory, which is the ability to absorb and remember verbal instructions.

Beef and Broccoli Stir Fry

A quick and tasty meal after a long day at work

Serves 4

Ingredients:

250g stir-fry beef strips
200g tenderstem broccoli – trimmed
1 red pepper – deseeded and sliced
4 mushrooms - sliced
1 onion – sliced
1 garlic clove – chopped
2 tablespoons extra virgin olive oil
100ml beef stock
4 tablespoons cold water

Marinade:
2 tablespoons Teriyaki marinade
1 teaspoon Chinese 5 spice
2 teaspoons honey
1 tablespoon light soy sauce

Method:

1. In a large bowl, combine the Teriyaki marinade with the Chinese 5 spice, light soy sauce and honey. Add the beef strips and stir well. Leave the beef in the marinade for at least 30 minutes.
2. Heat 1 tablespoon oil in a stir-fry pan. Sauté the onions and pepper for 2 minutes. Set aside.
3. Add the broccoli to the pan with 4 tablespoons of cold water and stir-fry the broccoli for 5 minutes. Set aside.
4. Using a slotted spoon, remove the beef from the marinade and keep the marinade to one side.
5. Heat 1 tablespoon oil and stir-fry the beef and garlic for 2 minutes.
6. Add the onions, pepper, mushrooms and broccoli to the pan and pour in the marinade and beef stock. Bring to the boil and cook until the sauce reduces and thickens.
7. Serve on a bed of steamed wholegrain brown rice or quinoa.

Chicken and Broccoli Bake

A hearty dinner perfect for a winter's day

Serves 2

Ingredients:

2 chicken breasts
1 medium onion – diced
150g tenderstem broccoli – trimmed
400ml vegetable stock or water
60ml dry white wine
100g cheddar cheese - grated

Cheese Sauce:
50g butter
50g wholegrain spelt flour
500ml whole milk
50g cheddar cheese - grated
Worcester sauce
Nutmeg
Pepper

Method:

1. Preheat oven to 180°C/160° Fan/Gas 4.
2. Place the chicken breasts, stock, wine and onion in a large pan and season well. Boil for 15 minutes until the chicken is cooked through. Strain and keep the chicken and onions aside.
3. Meanwhile, steam the broccoli for 5 minutes until it's tender but not soft. Drain and refresh under cold water.
4. Slice the chicken and arrange in a flat dish with the broccoli.
5. Make the sauce: melt the butter. Stir in the flour and cook for 3 minutes stirring constantly. Gradually, add the milk until it is all incorporated and the sauce is smooth. Add 50g grated cheese and continue to stir the sauce until it comes to the boil and starts to thicken. Season with a dash of Worcester sauce, a pinch of nutmeg and pepper.
6. Cover the chicken and broccoli with the cheese sauce.
7. Sprinkle over the grated cheese and bake in the oven for 20 minutes until the cheese is bubbling.
8. Serve with buttered baby potatoes.

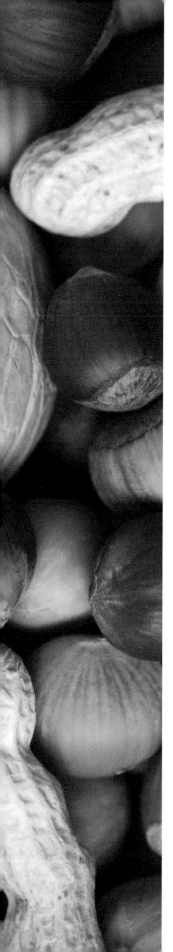

Nuts

Protect healthy brain function

Nuts are a rich source of vitamin E and omega-3 fatty acids, which are essential for the healthy functioning of the brain.

Studies suggest that a higher overall nut intake helps to prevent cognitive decline, especially in the elderly. As a person ages, their brain may be exposed to oxidative stress caused by free radicals. Vitamin E helps to protect cells from oxidative stress and therefore, reduces the risk of Alzheimer's and other degenerative brain diseases.

Walnuts are considered to be the best nut for brainpower because of their high concentration of docosahexaenoic acid (DHA). DHA is a type of Omega-3 fatty acid which is good for the cardiovascular system. Studies have shown that it helps to protect brain health in new born babies, as well as improving cognitive performance and preventing age-related cognitive decline. Furthermore, DHA plays a major role in preventing heart disease, arthritis and depression.

Walnut and Cranberry Cookies

A nutritious brain-boosting snack

Makes 12

Ingredients:

100g cranberries – halved
100g walnuts – chopped
100g dark chocolate chips
1 teaspoon orange essence
½ teaspoon bicarbonate of soda
100g butter
160g caster sugar
½ teaspoon salt
170g spelt flour
1 medium egg

Method:

1. Preheat oven to 180°C/160° Fan/Gas 4.
2. Cream the butter and sugar together in a bowl until the mixture is light and fluffy.
3. Slowly add the egg and orange essence.
4. Stir in the flour, salt and bicarbonate of soda, cranberries, walnuts and chocolate chips and mix well.
5. Chill the dough in a covered bowl in the fridge for 30 minutes.
6. Line 2 large baking trays with greaseproof paper.
7. Divide the dough into 12 balls and place them 5cm apart on the baking trays. Shape into flat rounds.
8. Bake for 20-25 minutes until golden brown. Cool on a wire tray.

Banana and Walnut Loaf

A family favourite

Serves 6

Ingredients:

120g butter
120ml maple syrup
1 egg - beaten
2 ripe bananas – coarsely mashed
3 tablespoons full-fat milk
250g wholegrain spelt flour
1 teaspoon bicarbonate of soda
½ teaspoon baking powder
50g walnuts – chopped

Method:

1. Preheat oven to 180°C/160° Fan/Gas 4.
2. Line a loaf tin (11cm x 18cm) with greaseproof paper.
3. Melt the butter.
4. Put the butter, maple syrup, egg, milk and bananas into a large bowl beat until mixed.
5. Mix together the flour, walnuts, bicarbonate of soda and baking powder and gently stir in the banana mixture.
6. Pour into the loaf tin and bake for 45 minutes until golden brown and cooked in the middle.

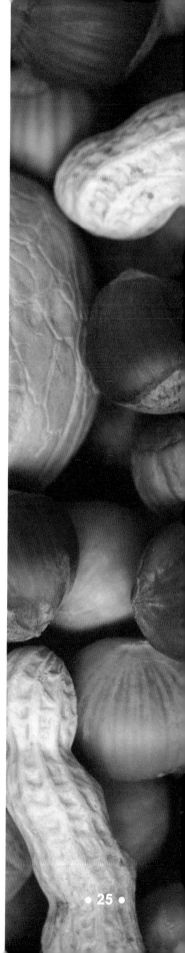

Tomatoes

Protect the brain from damage

Carotenoids – the nutrient found in bright red and orange vegetables – is known to improve cognitive functioning and memory.

The antioxidant, lycopene, is one of the most powerful carotenoids, which helps to protect against cell damage. It is the natural pigment that gives some vegetables and fruits their red colour and is found in high doses in the skin of tomatoes.

Lycopene eliminates free radicals and thereby, helps to protect the brain from depression-causing inflammation. This is the main reason why the increased consumption of lycopene-rich food is a universal health recommendation.

Research shows that cooking tomatoes enhance the effect that lycopene has on gut bacteria by increasing its absorption in the gut.

Lycopene is a fat-soluble nutrient, so for maximum benefit, it with foods rich in healthy fats like extra virgin olive oil.

Shakshuka

Delicious served for brunch or dinner

Serves 2

Ingredients:

1 tablespoon extra virgin olive oil
1 large onion – sliced
1 red pepper – sliced
1 green pepper – sliced
1 garlic clove – crushed
½ teaspoon turmeric
½ teaspoon curry powder
4 teaspoon smoked paprika
1 tablespoon tomato purée
2 teaspoons mixed herbs
2 x 400g tins tomatoes
4 eggs

Method:

1. Heat the oil in a large frying pan and stir fry the onion, pepper and garlic for 5 minutes until softened.
2. Stir in the spices and add the tomato purée, tomatoes and herbs. Simmer gently for 10 minutes to reduce the liquid. It should be moist but not dry or runny.
3. Make 4 small holes in the sauce and break an egg into each hole.
4. Cook the mixture until the egg whites set but the yolks are still runny.
5. Serve with warm pitta bread.

Serving Suggestion:

- Sprinkle with crumbled feta cheese.

Roasted Red Pepper and Tomato Soup

The ultimate comfort soup

Serves 4

Ingredients:

2 red peppers – deseeded and sliced into quarters
1 large onion – chopped
2 medium carrots – sliced
1kg fresh tomatoes – halved
2 tablespoons extra virgin olive oil
1 garlic clove – chopped
1½ tablespoons tomato purée
1 tablespoon tomato ketchup
650ml vegetable stock

Method:

1. Preheat oven to 180°C/160° Fan/Gas 4.
2. Place the peppers into a shallow roasting tin and brush with 1 tablespoon oil. Roast for 15 minutes until tender. Remove excess oil with kitchen paper and chop into chunks.
3. Heat the remaining oil in a large pan and sauté the onion, carrots and garlic until softened.
4. Stir in the tomato purée and ketchup.
5. Add the roasted peppers and tomatoes to the pan with the stock.
6. Simmer gently for 30 minutes until the tomatoes are soft.
7. Blend the soup in a food blender until smooth.
8. Serve with chunky slices of warm wholegrain bread.

Avocado

The powerhouse food

The avocado is known as the powerhouse food because it provides a multitude of health benefits beyond basic nutrition.

Avocados are packed with monosaturated fats, which help keep your blood sugar levels stable and make your skin glow. Monounsaturated fats support the production of acetylcholine, which is the brain chemical involved in memory and learning. Although the brain normally uses glucose for energy, it will happily burn healthy fats as a source of 'super fuel.'

Avocados also contain vitamin K and folate, which help prevent blood clots in the brain, thereby protecting against stroke. Furthermore, they are rich in vitamin B and vitamin C and have the highest protein and lowest sugar content of all other fruits. In addition, they are high in the amino acid tyrosine, which is the brain chemical responsible for keeping you motivated and focused.

However, avocados are also high in calories, so restrict consumption to a maximum of one avocado per day.

Spaghetti with Avocado Pesto, Tomato & Prawns

A zesty and spicy quick supper dish

Serves 4

Ingredients:

1 pack wholegrain spaghetti
1 ripe avocado - chopped
Handful of fresh basil leaves
30g pine nuts
1 tablespoons lemon juice
4 tablespoons extra virgin olive oil
1 garlic cloves – chopped
25g parmesan cheese – grated
150g cooked king prawns
8 cherry tomatoes

Method:

1. Blend together the avocado, basil, pine nuts, garlic, parmesan cheese and lemon juice. Add 4 tablespoons olive oil and process until smooth.
2. Meanwhile, boil the spaghetti until al dente. Drain.
3. Place the cooked spaghetti in a large bowl and mix in the pesto mixture. Add the prawns and stir through. Season well.
4. Serve topped with cherry tomatoes and a sprinkling of parmesan cheese. Delicious with warm ciabatta bread.

Avocado and Tomato Bruschetta with Poached Egg

A quick and simple breakfast or lunch

Serves 2

Ingredients:

Ciabatta or sourdough bread
8 cherry tomatoes - halved
1 ripe avocado - sliced
4 basil leaves - chopped
Extra virgin olive oil
4 large eggs

Method:

1. Preheat grill.
2. Slice the bread into 4 thick slices and place on a non-stick baking tray. Drizzle olive oil over the top. Bake until the bread is golden and crispy. Remove from the oven and arrange on a plate.
3. Mix the tomatoes and basil together in a bowl.
4. Evenly spread the avocado slices on top of the bread.
5. Add a layer of tomatoes.
6. Meanwhile, poach the eggs in a pan of water. Drain the eggs on kitchen paper to remove excess water.
7. Place the eggs on top of the tomatoes and season with pepper.

Serving Suggestion:

• Serve with a side of smoked salmon.

Dark Chocolate

Indulge your brain

The cacao in dark chocolate contains over 300 chemical compounds, one of which is an antioxidant called flavonoids, which are good for brain health. Oxidative stress is a major cause of age-related mental decline and brain diseases, so antioxidants are vital to help improve memory and cognitive functioning by stimulating blood flow to the brain. Furthermore, flavonoids promote brain plasticity and help brain cells to live longer.

Chocolate is also great source of tryptophan, which helps the body to produce the 'happy chemical' serotonin, which boosts happiness and well-being. It also contains anandamide, a naturally-occurring neurotransmitter which is often called the 'bliss molecule'. Anandamide binds to the same receptors as tetrahydrocannabinol, which is the main psychoactive component in marijuana. Furthermore, dark chocolate contains the 'love drug', phenylethylamine, which stimulates the feelings of love and the 'buzz' that is associated with being in love.

* Eat good quality dark chocolate which contains at least 70 percent cacao

Chocolate Orange Mousse

Indulge your brain in dark chocolate

Serves 4

Ingredients:

100g dark chocolate (minimum 75% cocoa solids)
4 large egg whites
50g Greek yogurt
1 tablespoon caster sugar
1 teaspoon orange essence

Method:

1. Melt the chocolate in the microwave or in a bowl set in a pan over boiling water. Remove from the heat and allow to cool slightly.
2. Add the orange essence.
3. Place the egg whites in a clean bowl and whisk to medium-stiff peaks. Add the sugar and continue to whisk until thoroughly mixed.
4. Stir the yogurt into the chocolate until combined.
5. Carefully fold the egg whites into the chocolate mixture until mixed.
6. Divide the mousse into 4 ramekin dishes. Chill for at least 4 hours before serving.

Chocolate Chip Muffins

The ultimate protein-packed brain snack

Makes 12-15 muffins

Ingredients:

300g plain flour
1 tablespoon baking powder
½ teaspoon baking soda
65g caster sugar
2 eggs
150ml extra virgin olive oil
200g natural Greek yogurt
60ml full-fat milk
1 teaspoon vanilla essence
150g dark chocolate chips

Method:

1. Preheat oven to 180°C/160° Fan/Gas 4.
2. Line the muffin tray with muffin cases.
3. Put the flour, baking powder, baking soda and sugar into a large bowl.
4. Whisk the egg and mix in the oil, yogurt, milk and vanilla essence.
5. Pour the egg mixture into the flour mix and stir until combined to make a batter. Don't overmix.
6. Fold the chocolate chips into the batter.
7. Fill the muffin cases with the batter.
8. Bake for 20-25 minutes until the muffins are golden and cooked through (put a skewer into the center of a muffin and if it comes out clean, the muffins are cooked). Can be eaten warm or cold.

Serving Suggestion:

- Serve with a side of blueberry jam (see recipe on page 9).

Whole Grains

Keep your brain active and alert

Your brain uses 20 percent of the energy in your body, so it the energy supply is insufficient, you may experience memory problems, tiredness and lack of concentration. Therefore, it's vitally important to provide your brain with a steady supply of nutritious fuel to keep your brain active and alert. Eating a diet rich in low glycemic-index (GI) foods like wholegrains, release glucose slowly into the bloodstream, which helps to boost mental alertness throughout the day.

Whole grains contain B vitamins, which play an important role in brain health. Vitamins B1 (thiamine), B2 (riboflavin), B3 (niacin), B5 (pantothenic acid), B6 (pyridoxine), B7 (biotin), B9 (folic acid) and B12 (cobalamin), perform a range of essential roles to keep your brain in peak condition. They help to prevent dementia, boost the production of neurotransmitters – chemicals that deliver messages between the brain and body - and enhance blood flow to the brain.

Therefore, eat a diet rich in whole grain foods including whole oats, whole wheat, spelt, quinoa, whole grain bread and pasta and brown rice.

Spicy Chicken Rice

A quick and easy one pot family supper

Serves 4

Ingredients:

1 medium onion – diced
1 red pepper – sliced thinly
1 garlic clove – crushed
2 teaspoons turmeric powder
1 teaspoon curry powder
400g tin tomatoes
250g wholegrain brown rice
450ml stock
300g chicken – chopped into bitesize pieces
2 tablespoons extra virgin olive oil
Chilli flakes

Method:

1. Place the chicken in a bowl and add the turmeric and curry powder. Mix well.
2. In a deep stir-fry pan, sauté the onions until soft. Add the pepper and garlic and fry on a medium heat for 3 minutes.
3. Add the tomatoes, stock, rice, chilli flakes and chicken. Stir well.
4. Cover the pan and simmer for 20 minutes or until all the liquid has been absorbed. Stir occasionally to prevent the rice from sticking to the pan.
5. Season well and serve with warm wholegrain naan bread or pitta.

Blueberry Parfait

Wake Up Your Brain

Serves 1

Ingredients:

150g Greek yogurt
90g granola
½ teaspoon chia seeds
100g fresh blueberries
2 tablespoons blueberry jam (recipe on page 9)

Method:

1. Spoon a layer of yogurt into the bottom of a small mason jar.
2. Add a layer of blueberry jam.
3. Add another layer of yogurt and sprinkle with fresh blueberries and chia seeds.
4. Add a final layer of yogurt and top with the granola.
5. Refrigerate overnight and serve.

Serving Suggestion:

• Substitute the blueberries for raspberries, strawberries or a mix.

Turmeric

The spice of life

Turmeric is a deep-yellow spice and is one of the main spices in curry powder because of its rich flavour. Turmeric powder is made from the dried root of the Curcuma longa plant.

Turmeric contains curcuminoids, the most active of which is curcumin. Curcumin is a powerful antioxidant and anti-inflammatory and has several benefits for the brain, including helping with memory and alleviating stress and anxiety.

Alzheimer's disease results in the build-up of the protein amyloid-beta, which forms clumps known as amyloid plaques. Studies show that turmeric can cross the blood-brain barrier to help clear amyloid plaques and thereby help to improve the memory of Alzheimer's patients.

Turmeric also helps to ease depression and improve mood by boosting serotonin and dopamine. It supports the working memory and helps maintain calmness and an ability to cope with stress and anxiety.

Sweet Potato Wedges

A spicy accompaniment to fish dishes

Serves 4

Ingredients:

1kg sweet potatoes - washed
1 teaspoon turmeric
2 tablespoons extra virgin olive oil

Method:

1. Cut the potatoes into wedges leaving the skin on.
2. Put the potatoes into a pan of cold water and add the turmeric. Bring to the boil and simmer for 5 minutes. Drain and leave to cool. (This can be done the day before and the potatoes left in the refrigerator overnight).
3. Preheat oven to 200°C/180° Fan/Gas 6.
4. Toss the potatoes in 1 tablespoon oil. Heat the remaining oil in a shallow roasting tin.
5. Add the potatoes to the hot oil and coat the wedges until covered.
6. Arrange the wedges in a single layer in the tin.
7. Roast for 30 minutes.
8. Turn the wedges and cook for another 15 minutes until crisp and golden.

Serving Suggestions:

- Substitute the sweet potatoes for Maris Piper potatoes.
- Serve with baked fish (recipe on page 13).

Golden Vegetable Curry

Spice Up Your Brain

Serves 2

Ingredients:

2 large carrots - sliced
2 courgettes - sliced
1 red pepper – deseeded and sliced
1 large onion – chopped
1 sweet potato – chopped into small chunks
100g tenderstem broccoli – washed and trimmed
10 cherry tomatoes - halved
400ml coconut milk
2 teaspoons turmeric
1 teaspoon curry powder
1 teaspoon chilli flakes
1 tablespoon extra virgin olive oil

Method:

1. Heat the oil in a deep pan or pot and gently sauté the onions for 3 minutes until translucent.
2. Add the vegetables, and with the lid on the pan, steam on a low heat for 3 minutes.
3. Stir in the coconut milk, spices and chilli flakes and simmer for 20-25 minutes until the sweet potato is tender.
4. Remove the pan from the heat and season well.
5. Serve with wholegrain rice or quinoa and whole wheat naan bread or pitta.

To my beautiful daughters

♡ ♡

About the Author

Jayne Cormie is the founder and managing director of The Thinking Business Limited; a global training and consulting company specialising in thinking skills and storytelling.

Prior to launching The Thinking Business in 2000, Jayne spent many years in the FMCG industry as a marketing manager working for several food companies including United Biscuits and Heinz. Her corporate roles involved developing new product ideas and developing creative marketing campaigns for major brands.

She has a Bachelor of Arts Honours degree in Education specialising in Food and Nutrition and a Master of Business Administration degree. She is a licensed Buzan instructor in Mind Mapping, Speed Reading and Memory Skills and Graduate of the Disney Institute's Creativity & Innovation Programme.

www.thethinkingbusiness.com

Disclaimer

The information in this document is provided for general information only, and should never be used as a substitute for the medical advice of your own doctor or any other health care professional. If you have any concerns about your health, you should contact your local doctor or other qualified healthcare professional.

Copyright Notice

Printed in Poland
by Amazon Fulfillment
Poland Sp. z o.o., Wrocław

62117994R00028